FIELD REQUIEM

Sheri Benning grew up on a farm in central Saskatchewan, Canada. She's the author of *The Season's Vagrant Light* (Carcanet Press), as well as *Thin Moon Psalm* (Brick Books) and *Earth After Rain* (Thistledown Press) published in Canada. Her poems, essays and short stories have appeared in North American, British and European journals and anthologies, most recently *The Paris Review*, *Times Literary Supplement* and *PN Review*. Benning completed a PhD at the University of Glasgow and currently lives in Saskatchewan, where she teaches.

ALSO BY SHERI BENNING FROM CARCANET

The Season's Vagrant Light

Field Requiem

SHERI BENNING

CARCANET POETRY

First published in Great Britain in 2021 by
Carcanet
Alliance House, 30 Cross Street
Manchester, M2 7AQ
www.carcanet.co.uk

A CIP catalogue record for this book is
available from the British Library.

ISBN 978 1 80017 151 0

Book design by Andrew Latimer

The publisher acknowledges financial
assistance from Arts Council England.

CONTENTS

What's coming
won't be human if it has
no ghost.

– Jan Zwicky, 'Depth'

FIELD REQUIEM

All of it –
the house in the village.
The house in the side of a hill.

The farm by Mariupol,
the farm by Mount Carmel,
Wolverine Creek, Bay Trail.

The abbey where we planted
a copse of blue spruce.
The blue spruce.

Pit dug. Fire lit. Ripe fields
pulse with light and shadow.
Clouds rush overhead.

℟ *Blessed is the field as it burns.*

I

Exaudi orationem meam ~

WINTER SLEEP

Luke 19:11

Wheat threshed, casks of cherries, plums,
boiled melon, beef tallow, pig bladders blown
and tossed by children, mothers stirring stock,
kidneys, hearts pressed with aspic,

casings scraped and stuffed, allspice, cloves.
Fields bare, packed clay, porcelain sheen,
the long winter sleep. In my dream,
I wake and the village is empty,

coal smouldering, acacia shadows on snow.
Second sons, sow-thistle, the first to go.
In my dream, I wake to chaff and dust,
a war lost, harvest thrown down,

grain scattered on the temple floor.
In my dream, I wake hungry, an ocean away
in a hut hollowed out of the side of a hill, Black Sea
salt in my mouth. Wild onion, sage,

hawkweed, prickly rose, ploughed
dirt worked thin as smoke, poplar scrub
felled and bucked into windrows to make way for
electric blooms, Monsanto Roundup Ready Canola.

What we had wasn't enough. Silk, balsam,
communal granaries full. We were told to take
what the master had given us and multiply it tenfold.
In my dream, I wake in the attic bedroom

of a mail-order farmhouse. 160 acres seeded
in barley and oats. A few brood hens, five head of cattle,
three-hitch binder, a trotter, two heavy horses. We were told
to take what we did not lay down, reap what we did not sow.

I wake to 6000 acres, high clearance sprayers
with 140-foot booms. Sulfur, phosphorus, nitrogen,
potash. Harvest done by drone. Yields downloaded
into $750 000 air seeders come spring. We were told –

to those who have, more will be given.
Viterra's actuaries betting on futures markets,
brokering grain they don't own. We were told
those with nothing, even that will be taken away.

Just look at those who stayed –
in my dream, the men from Grünau, found
heads down, shoulder-to-shoulder, tongues
nailed to the dining table.

Or Alex Saretzky from Tiegenort,
blood pouring from his wrists, hands cut off
by Makhnovists requisitioning his cattle.
In my dream we tell these stories

to our babies in their cradles.
The lesson of the parable? What good is your labour
if the fruit doesn't grow and grow and grow?
I wake in the hip-roof barn,

and where we hang the throat-cut animal,
men dangle. Hailstorm, flood, drought.
Interest rates. Debt loads. Go big, or
get out.

PLAINSONG

Driving home from Uncle Richard's,
in the backseat with my brother and sister -
weft of limbs, pearlescence of moonlit skin,
shift and fall of their breath.

My face against the car window to watch stars, and every mile
a farm, yard-lights,
a voice in plainsong -

after feeding the cattle, Dave Saretzky stepping into his porch,
borscht warming on the stove,
hambone, pepper, cloves.
She's tucking in their youngest boy,
her palm on his feverish cheek.
After, she and Dave will sleep, in the space their bodies have learned
to make from years of sharing
blood, spit, loam -

Blink of frost on wheat stalks, fields left in stubble to snare
October's first snow-squall, the tip of dad's cigarette,
knots of smoke, mother singing low to the radio,
the gypsy-light of stars and farms,
a raw harmony

like the dark wave of geese lifting off the slough just east of our barns.
Their winter homing, a folksong for the journey
to where flesh might belong.

Our farm's sold. Dave's too. Uncle Richard died seventeen years ago.
Only now the light of this memory reaches me.

MINOR DOXOLOGY

I

Circle of light on the village street
from his kitchen window where he stands
in the slowing breath of nightfall,

stares through that cold fire
into sifting shadow: dusk-blue
snow banked against the porch,

and beyond the row of houses,
evergreens in daguerreotype
darkening on winter fields.

The galvanised taste of chores
rises in his mouth: well-water,
dander, frost and straw.

And because place calls to place
inside us, he is seventy in the kitchen,
even as he is twelve in the farmyard,

midway between house and barn,
metal pail of new milk, quarter moon,
spilled oats, early stars.

II

Dust and husk shrouded sun, heavy
on horizon. Rosehips, alder catkins –
the colour of that boy's blood scabbing
in his road crew sleeping bag.

Place calls to place,
so though he's forty-two, walking in
from chores, he's twenty-four, heading north
to drive front-loader for Lux Construction.

The car passed him outside Paddockwood,
eighty miles an hour when it hit the approach.
Rolled end-over-end. First on the scene.
There are three of us –

the kid with glass in his hair screamed.
One wedged in the backseat, still breathing.
Fifty feet from impact, the other, creek of blood
gurgling from his mouth. The boy was drowning

so he took him in his arms, slid him around,
head above heart. Last night, his daughter found it
in the basement closet. Ferric wings, trace fossil
of the boy bleeding out. Now,

between house and barn, he holds the dying boy
in a ditch. Their bodies' shiver against each other
as they wait for the ambulance. Dusk frost,
late August, night coming on.

III

Sparrows on the bail stack,
his dad's Mossberg cocked, Ronnie Suchan
climbed the corral fence for a better shot.
Honeyed smell of manure and hay,

air like glass, Spring's freeze and thaw,
Ronnie slipped from the icy slat, pitched the rifle.
Did he see the barrel pointed at his face?
Place, in its mercy, holds all:

Ronnie Suchan on his back in ryegrass
and downy brome, eyes wide to the cloudless
Lenten sky, and his best friend who,
sixty years later, pauses to breathe

April's snow mould, crocuses, aspen sap,
and to touch the black blister, winter-killed
saskatoon, as if to put his finger
on Ronnie's wound.

IV

The summer he was eighteen he drove dozer through
poplar bluffs, cleared fields for farmers, $1.50 an hour,
open air cab, face lashed by willow and juneberry branches,

must of geosmin and spore from never-before dug dirt.
Dun flash of mud hens or grouse, winterfat, loosestrife,
golden rod, nodding thistle caught in the bushrake.

If awake, he felled brush. But once,
Corporal Rawlings stopped him. *Can you handle a gun?*
Highway check-stop, provincial manhunt,

the Peterson children shot in their beds, their father
found slumped by the kitchen door, mother and infant
beneath an open window. *Rules are simple,*

stay behind the police car. If you hear something, shoot.
Hours, crouched behind Rawling's cruiser at the junction
of 20 & 16. Ears unplugged from the shrieking machine,

forearms flexed, he listened to the field's fricative silence,
dry rub of bush crickets and two-striped grasshoppers,
velvet stutter, a Great Horned owl, volley of coyote calls.

Night pressing down, heat of the day rose
in mist, like sighing breath, like leavening
bread, and it filled him.

EXTREME UNCTION

Four years old, he wants to help the hired man
throw rocks down the dry well to close it.
The wagon's steel wheel rolls

across his little-boy stomach. Nausea
and the fever dream begins – he opens his eyes,
the hired man screams, *I never saw him!*

Guts squeezed into lower belly and scrotum.
He opens his eyes and the white mask says,
Breathe deep, smell of rubber,

alfalfa, sweet clover. He falls in
and the bright star above him grows
smaller, smaller. He calls for his mother,

hatchling shrieks swallowed by dank dirt.
He opens his eyes, pyx and burse.
Oil, balsam, wooden crucifix

swings from the priest's neck as he thumbs
cross on forehead, extreme unction.
July heat. Leather girdle. Weeks and weeks,

nuns sweep in and out with sips of water.
Hook of moon lifts above the hospital's hedge
of willow, poplar. He opens his eyes

and he's twenty-seven, pantleg caught
in the grain auger. He opens his eyes
as his car's hood rolls over top him.

He opens his eyes, chest cracked,
heart attack, lung shadow. Safety latch
popped on the hydraulic jack,

face bandaged, he opens his eyes
to wet dark, calls and calls
from the well's bottom.

More than sixty years trapped.
I wait by his hospital bed, hold his hand.
Seventh son. No one comes for him.

INTERCESSION

My father with the trick heart stops
while we walk the hot city, says,
Look at the beautiful roses –

yellow and pink blooms growing
through someone's garden fence,
and I want to give him armfuls,

the scent reminding me of something
like childhood, which comes apart
in my hands, petals crushed

by wind and rain. Tobacco, diesel, his palms
stained, rough-cut wood, but when I was a girl
and he wiped my face, held a tissue to my nose?

He touches a blossom, says *Look –*
and I want to give him acres, fields,
for when he was a child and no one believed,

for when he dropped out of school,
worked road crew, north of Muskoday,
a bouncer at the Patricia Hotel, Saskatoon.

Hands scarred by beatings, but
when he touches a petal, my cheek?
His heart runs too fast, too slow.

Doctors can't figure out the trick,
so we sit on a park bench,
hailstorm light in the east.

BURY WHAT'S LEFT

We thrash through foxtail, fescue,
volunteer canola, crested wheat,
to the back forty, a pit where we toss

what we can't take – metal bedframe,
school reports, bread clips, elastic bands,
water bottle lids. Ex indumentis.

Dad and I are here to bury what's left.
To lock the house. Machinery sold –
4490 Case IH, John Deere backhoe,

swather, seed hawk, heavy harrow,
International grain truck, grid road
through floorboards, barley chaff itch.

Neighbours picked the bones, buckets
of hose clamps, crop lifters, nuts, bolts.
I spent the winter away. I want to ask

what happened to the dogs? Skinny
and head shy when we got them,
an ad in the *Western Producer*,

by the end of summer, they followed Dad
around the yard, small chat between changing
cultivator shovels, sprayer nozzles.

Once he found the blonde one whimpering
behind the grain bins, snout and hindquarters
full of porcupine quills.

Dad pinned him to the dirt, went to work with pliers.
I could hear their cries from inside the house.
Every day, until the dog could limp,

Dad carried him from his wallow in the barn
to his favourite spot, willow shade by the fuel tanks.
Who'd want them? Old for German Shepherds,

three-legged, diabetic, blind.
You'd never get them in the truck. Too territorial.
And the guy who bought our land?

Farms 12 000 acres. What does he care
about two half-dead shepherds?
He'd let them starve.

I want to ask, but the sky's heavy
with shifting weather. Besides,
I know the answer. Someone had to

lay them in the reliquary, swathe them
in linen and spice, horsemint, silver sage,
axle-greased polycotton, shop rags.

COMPLINE

St Peter's Abbey, Muenster Saskatchewan

. . . Or do we call it memory
because we cannot bear to say
the longed-for that did not come to pass.
– Jan Zwicky, 'Kinderszenen'

Strange to find oneself at the end of it all.
Fog frozen in aspens and alders along Wolverine Creek,
snow-shawled cattail reeds, chokecherry branches,

scabbed berries starred with frost. I walk to the copse
of blue spruce planted at the abbey by my long-dead uncle,
Fr. Xavier, eighty years ago. Jackrabbit tracks and I remember

my dad, ten years old, snaring in Joe Takács's pasture.
Twelve cents a pelt from Hubert Kopp, the furrier,
who fed the carcasses to his minks.

Bells cut winter air, call monks to prayer,
divine office uninterrupted since Ascension Thursday,
1903, the abbey founded to tend to the new Catholic colony.

Sometimes my dad skinned one in Takács's scrub. Split ribs,
scooped guts. Laddy, his dog, bouncing for the musk of blood.
Bells in spruce-filtered dusk and I remember Joe Takács,

clank of his axe, felling sickly poplars to heat his house,
to escape the war stuck in his head, left nostril ripped
by a Russian bayonet. He hid for days up a tree,

licked dew from leaves, until the enemy's retreat. Remember
my dad, rinsing hindquarters in a willow-netted drift.
Quick fire, sweet balsam, gamey mouthful of meat.

Late for supper chores, still scared by shadows
in the dark barn, he rested his cheek against the hull
of her hips, the cow he milked named Beauty,

smell of dander and chaff. Joe Takács,
kids grown, wife buried, sold up, moved to the abbey,
worked with the monks on their farm until his death.

Now, fields are cropped based on the half-life
of herbicides, commodity markets, fertiliser costs.
Snow, surgical drapes, amnesic-white.

No scrub. No pasture. Every acre scraped.
Remember my dad, walking to the farmyard –
new moon, ghosts of breath. Remember Joe Takács

cleaning stalls, hauling hay after morning mass,
while somewhere in Hungary still hiding in a tree. Now,
there are only twelve monks left, barns and gardens empty.

These are not my memories. Unless
memory is what we call the longed-for.
What did not come to pass.

II

eleison

SLAUGHTER

I thought there'd always be a lustre of time,
rich and slick like the animal's oiled hide. I shot one

for its leather, another for the tender meat of its spine.
One more for the fetor of estrus in fur, for its tree-rubbed horns,

the spice of cedar and pine. One for its muscled gallop,
the crack and the echo, the arc of the bullet shattering prairie night.

For the shocked silence after the last steamed snort and cry. I stood
high on a pile of bones, sun-sucked skulls, rifle erect at my side.

From a thicket of poplar and birch, the coyotes' keen rose,
cut through industry's metallic reek, shroud of gunsmoke.

Drunk and glutted, sweet grease on my lips, I never thought
that my careless slaughter would lead to such hunger –

thin hospital flannel wrapped around my shoulders
by some kind nurse – that I'd be here,

trying to atone for that wasted flesh,
keeping vigil at your bedside.

NATIVITY

After it all, November sky
over our razed fields,

a boiled bone, a bloodless lung.
Flax stubble, ash and spent wicks.

Thin smoke in the middle distance,
as though harvest was a war –

at thaw the armor will roll out, dig in,
begin again. But then the bluing eastern horizon,

sheen on worn iron, and suddenly snow fell.
Hip-high drifts blown against the garden fence.

You wanted to walk outside so I found our winter coats
in the basement closet, still holding our shape.

I thought of matted pasture grass
where a deer has lain. Sleeping

spoor of the body woven into wool –
dust, old hair, sweat, cologne. In the snow

we were made new. Snow, a cool chrism
on last season's wounds. You laughed

as a child can, unburdened,
mouth open, face to sky,

snow melting on your tongue.
Head shorn from surgery,

in your brown coat you looked like a happy monk,
so I joined you. Dizzy with praise and falling

snow, we sank to our knees, rose
again into the frosted clouds of our breath,

and breathed in those small ghosts
of who we were just moments before.

ALMS

I held your hand when the doctor spoke
for fear that your touch was the last I'd feel
before the weather cools – your life falling
from you plain as leaves from the poplars
that shelter our farm. Hungry, wearing
borrowed clothes, after the doctor left,
I crouched in a stairwell, wept. My eyes,
green gloss on a copper begging-bowl.
Most hurried past. A few did not turn away.
Alms, simple food, bright coin of their gaze.

KELLY WIENS
(1978–2018)

For the long-limbed dance of you,
    your hair in my mouth, rye-and-coke breath, drugstore shampoo,
            baby-powder sweet stink of you.

                                                The nicotine buzz,
            ice off the lake, jump in, eyes shut, nose plugged,
                        freshwater-on-skin scream of you.

                                    Bar-closed drive home, 2am, Highway 5,
    Quill Lake, Watson, Englefeld. In the rearview, you:
passed out, head in Faye's lap, feel of your pulse,
the aurora borealis of you.

                                    My first spring in the city,
our friend Lindsay knocked on my door, held out her hands:
a mango. I'd never seen one before.

Dust and crushed paper,
winter swept into kitchen corners,
she cut the leather rind, the soft fruit. Juice down her wrists,

                                    flesh on knife tip, dusk light
            lengthening minute by minute. The shock of it
in our mouths, cut clover, our mothers' perfume.
                                                            O Kelly,

for the flora of you: the kingdom, the phylum,
sugar, yeast, virus, spore
of you.

PENTECOST

A crack in the dam of late-winter sky,
light syrups the field, deer-hide blonde,
last year's crop, legumes, rich tilth,
grainy snow. Soon,

the furred petals of crocus.
Soon, the meadowlark's ostinato,
Cattail gauze, blown poplar seed,
sun in a woman's silk blouse.

You want to walk after a season of sleep.
And I remember you, doctor on either side,
sitting up for the first time. Shaved head,
you couldn't focus your eyes,

the robin embryo I found in our caraganas –
hatched, raw, fallen from the nest. But now
we are walking, thinking about our dead.
They nudge us softly,

like how our shepherds nose our thighs
when they want to be fed. The dogs run
in the ditch beside us, chasing scent,
gophers, moles, jackrabbits.

You don't have to worry – you said
in the night-tent, your hospital room,
voice scarred by newly removed tubes.

Eyes closed, you held my hand.
Even if you died, you would've never left –
they're with me. Like in a dream? I asked.

No. Here. What keeps us separate from death,
thin as a curtain between beds. To your left,
an old woman purred. Jaw wide,

steady motor of sleep. Kitty corner,
a woman who spoke in tongues. At night,
tired of being locked in a language of one,

she'd weep. Once, you climbed your guardrail,
sat beside the crying woman, stroked her back.
How many nights did you drift to me?

Hold me to your chest? Half asleep, milk,
or its memory, in your nightshirt.
We reach the empty yard, poplar shelterbelt,

branches, capillaries, the sky's pulsing heart.
Steaming fields, lick of flames. We know we escaped
nothing. But my god. The glory

of reprieve. *Listen,*
you call over a rising wind –
lifting from stubble, wave upon wave,
snow geese.

VESPERS

Hanks of ditch grass – fescue, brome, spear,
bluestem, blue-eyed, hip-high sow-thistle,
coyote-scat cairns, creeping smoke
of pasture sage, Chipping Sparrow drone.

After supper, summer, we'd walk
to St Scholastica's abandoned cemetery,
southeast of the farm. You showed us where
parishioners peeled back the thick loam,

tucked in your nameless sisters. No stones
to mark graves, but a wind-gnawed cross,
prickly rose budding in sun-cured cow shit,
tiger lilies, lit flares.

*

Oldest daughter, you prepared your sisters
for earth, wiped vernix from fists and eyes.
Washed clean of birth's grease, sebum and cilia,
like the vegetable seeds you steeped
to soften husks. Infant skulls, allium bulbs,
pulp rich and sweet with utero-dreams
of silver light in birch leaves,
of grasses low suss.

*

At the end, you thought there'd be an emissary.
Dawn-grey feathers and webbing pressed
against your care home window.
Like in that sepia story –

another sister, the Spanish flu. Coal-eyed, ripe
with fever, bound in sweat's tight lace, she begged
for an open window. January prairie,
a knife held to throat.

Last deep swallow of frost, milk-blue
shadows of snow, she gave up the ghost,
you told us with the conviction of your faith,
crosshairs away from superstition.

*

Creek-cool breeze sliced the ammonia
perfume of flowering canola, yellow blooms
in the black light of thunderstorm, kick and snort,
horses mounting on the horizon.

No flash of grief when you stood
on the soil of your sisters, fine ribs
stripped of marrow and sap, plaited by dirt
into alms-baskets, heirloom pearl.

*

You're buried off Highway 5, the graveyard
east of town. Shelterbelt of caraganas
stunted by car exhaust.

Case IH dealership, bulk fuel, feed mill,
Peavey Mart – surrounding fields paved
for agroindustry parking lots.

We'll gather in dusk's blue hour, take up your bones,
walk through mist and cricket throb rising
from sloughs, the pasture's low spots,

deliver you to the braid of your sisters.
Hatched moon caught in blossoming poplars.
A canticle of horned owls, nighthawks, grey thrush.

III

... I am writing this
not to recall our lives,
but to imagine them.

– Eavan Boland, 'First Year'

OF

Rosalie née Tobin. Twenty-six, 1983.
She sits in her used LTD Ford Station wagon,
Co-op parking lot. Marriage on the rocks,

parents soon dead – lung cancer, heart attack.
July thunderstorm in the south sky. Supercells bloom
behind the hockey rink, the gutted stockyard.

Three kids under five buckled in the backseat.
She can feel their stare on her sunburned shoulders,
knows they know

she's crying again, so she cranks the radio.
Carly Simon. *Clouds in my coffee, clouds in my coffee.*
Full-throttle, off-key, eyes in the rearview, she sings

until the kids sing, too. Shift in atmospheric pressure
years later, and a vein bursts. Left front temporal lobe.
She falls on their farmhouse porch.

Florescent hum in the basement room off ICU.
Kids grown, a surgeon shows them scans –
blood rolls, cumulonimbus, *clouds in my coffee,*

and hail ricochets off asphalt, ozone and petrichor,
they're holding hands again, making a break
for the cold grocery store, wet-haired, shrieking.

PONTEIX, SASKATCHEWAN: NOVEMBER, 1919

Black blizzard, wet lungs,
snow, sand, cytokine storm.

A rope around her husband's
waist, tethered to their porch.

Someone had to do the milking.
Someone had to feed the horses.

Camphor, mustard, turpentine,
wormwood. Nuns in shadow-habits

plaster her chest. A rope around her
husband's waist so she could drag him back.

Farmers conscripted to dig frozen dirt,
plant tuberous corpses. Train cars,

coffins cracked, a whole threshing crew
found dead near Roleau, southwest of Regina.

Blue fingers. Blue lips. Cyanosis. By noon
the next day they buried her husband.

A rope around his waist so he could drag her
into his unmarked grave, rhizomes of men.

Nuns in shadow-habits beat her
with hailstone-fists to break up phlegm.

A neighbour found them in the nest,
the marriage bed, Johanna née Visser and

her mewling litter, her skinny baby birds.
She thought she heard the shadow

nuns whisper, *how will we divvy up*
her daughters? when she grabbed the knife,

the serrated blade, hacked and
hacked at the fraying rope.

OF

Petronella née Klein, Nelly.
320 acres of smoke-thin dirt. Pleuritic lungs.
Gertrude, Anna, Wilhelmina, Katerina, Marie –

too many sisters. Baby birds.
Sweat-stained cotton. Dry pink tongues.
Father dead. Twelve head of cattle. An alkali well.

A mother who said she could do no right. So she left
school at the convent. Fifteen, 1928. Became a maid
for the rich French family in Ponteix.

Limestone. Sugar and egg whites, whipped.
Lace doilies on armrests. His hands beneath her skirt.
What was she supposed to do?

So she thought of the hard rain
of hooves, her horse at the farm, wind
pulling her rag curls loose.

She gave the baby to her mother. A boy.
One thing right. Five years later, Freddie died.
Hemorrhage. Kitchen table tonsillectomy.

His bones thickening, turning in her womb,
the Pietà of her girlish lap, at the end of her life
she wrote to Mina from Surrey –

even the simplest words are hard
there's so much I work to forget.

PONTEIX, SASKATCHEWAN: JULY 1929

Wilhelmina in a well, sour water
ankle high, a rope around her waist tied to the lip.
Mother leans in, her face, a moon, eclipses the glimpse
of blood-blister blue noon sky – *If you fall, I'll pull
you out.* Wilhelmina climbs the ladder down,

down, down, 35 feet, to mop spilled milk,
well-walls hung with butter and cream. At night,
Wilhelmina sleeps with her sisters in the steep attic,
a house of bleached bones. Bronchial tubes broken,
pneumonia-scarred lungs, she coughs,

coughs, coughs, *I'll pull you out,* and wakes
into scabland. Cacti, sage, glacial wash, constellations
of stone. Spring wheat like lace, four bushels an acre,
salt grass and sulphate sloughs. But before Mother
shouts, before the tug of the rope,

she dreams cherry blossom drifts, rain's cricket-hiss,
wet oil of earth. She swears for the rest of her life
that when she looked up from the deep, she could see
Sirius, Vega, Venus or Mars. Of course,
she could not.

OF

the baby, name lost. 1906. Spring born,
almond and blackthorn in bloom. Meadowsweet,
chickweed, petals of milk on her lips.

Spider-silk saliva from mouth to crabapple fists,
on Mother's lap, the train from Kiev to Minsk
after the last harvest in Tiegenort.

Teething, feverish, pinpricked cheeks, Mother sings
Kniereiter to distract – *bouncing, bouncing baby.*
Should you fall in the ditch, ravens will feast,
ravens will feast.

Bitter pip of sick picked up in Riga's quarantine. Soon
they will slip her little body into the Baltic, wrapped
in blue douppioni cut from Mother's wedding dress,

but now she conducts with waving fists, skeins of dawn
mist lift from feathergrass and knapweed by the tracks,
Mother's soft breath in the cradle of the train car –

bouncing, bouncing baby. Should you fall
in the sea, should you fall in the sea.
Ravens perch in witches'-broom
of passing oak and silver fir.

OF

Mathilde née Saretsky, Tillie. Sixteen, 1936,
bloody knuckles, ammonia reek, scrubbing floors,
washing sheets at the Pioneer Hotel,

twelve miles from the farm. As far away
as she could get. Left Mary, her older sister,
to care for their always-sick mother, the babies,

the shit and the piss, abscessed milk, hauling
water from pump to house, burning welts
beneath dresses from his leather belt.

On her knees, thin waist, cherry lipstick,
eyes like Spring runoff in Wolverine Creek,
tips in her *Player's* tobacco tin, she made it

to Edmonton, became a stewardess. Lied
about her age, married Hank, an artist,
a draft dodger from Holland –

starry nights, sunflowers, canals.
Paintings hung on walls. High on Vatican II,
Pedagogy of the Oppressed,

she quit her job at the airline to feed orphans
in Brazil. Nicaragua. Guatemala. El Salvador.
Cigarette smoke, *Vicks* candy, church hall

after mass (the anniversary of Óscar Romero,
at the altar, shot dead), her voice in my ear:
That woman who kissed me,

her husband didn't come home.
She found him in the street. San Salvador.
Death squads. Starving dogs. Fresh meat.

Every effort against injustice and sin
God desires. Demands. Blood, the price
of salvation, Romero's last homily like a bullet

in the chest. Wearing her Che Guevara sweatshirt,
the week she died (pneumonia, ninety-six)
she climbed a ladder to clean her eaves.

The last thing she said to me?
Cherry lipstick, cigarette smoke, cough candy,
squeezing my hands at my mother's bedside –
Believe. Believe.

OF

Amalia, neé Kobelsky. 1964.
Sisters Minnie and Beth on her front porch.
She hasn't seen them for more than thirty years

when at twenty she ran away from the farm
with the CP Rail section hand.
Before she draws breath,

a spaciousness, Beth's eyes the same
as rusted wheat, late autumn poplar leaves,
turned dirt, black currants, cold blades of frost.

The section hand was Protestant.
Might as well be dead,
last letter from her parents.

That night, her husband asleep, she steps out
onto their bungalow's back patio. New moon,
overcast, trapped light from the city horizon,

creek-bottom orange, when from the depthless
sky, the season's self-erasure,
the first heavy snow –

I don't know who she is.
I don't know who you're looking for,
she told her sisters as she closed the door.
Please go.

BEFORE

their collagen hives dried
and her bones cracked, the richness
of her belly and thighs, grave wax.

Before bile and iron frayed
her best summer dress. Before
the cancer diagnosis, the heart attack.

Before the first winter she lived in sod,
dug in to spear grass, wolf willow, aspen
roots, Arctic rose, whitetail scat,
slept in straw, drank snow.

Before weeks in steerage's salt
and heave. Before she said goodbye
to her mother in clouds of diesel steam,
the train platform in Mariupol.

Before Mother's letters stopped arriving.
Before fourteen babies opened her womb,
she was sixteen, 1890, a girl in Tiegenort,
holding her sister's hand in the still-

dark morning, processing through frozen
plum and pear trees, acacia hoarfrost canopy,
to church for *Maria Lichtmess.* Candlelit faces,
small moons, midway to equinox. Of

Regina Elizabeth née Metlewsky –
the spill of her teeth in dirt, taper flames,
sparks of wheat, embers of burnt offerings.

IF SHE DID NOT

wake in the night to her new sister's cry,
cracked seed, undone swaddling, husks
of their dead father's dream.

If she did not balm the baby's stiff belly
with mint and absinthe emulsified lard,
waxing crescent gleam in lamp-felted dark.

If she did not listen to Old Aunty
who said, *Let Mother rest.* Nine days in bed
for the bones to knit back. Poultice of thyme

so the womb will shed. Boil crocus,
rosehip and hyssop for cramps.
If you are scared, sing

'Nightmare, nightmare, you cannot enter –'
Mama's fast breath, brow hallowed
with sweat, the whites of her eyes,

moons veiled in cirrus. *If you are scared,*
come find me. If she did not slip out the door,
beyond the skirt of porchlight

into snow-sifted shadow. If she did not bend into
ice-whetted wind, and when she heard the keen,
the tightening noose of wolves,

if she did not curl up on frozen furrows,
cover her face with her hood, small sips of air
melting the fresh skiff, wheat stubble, cold dirt,

the warm muzzle's nudge, uric steam –
Nightmare, nightmare, not until you've swum the seas,
not until you've crossed the field. If she did not

get up. If she did not keep walking to brushstrokes
on the horizon, their neighbour's copse,
poplar, willow, birch.

OF

the swineherd on the sovkhoz,
Arkhangelsk Oblast, who steals handfuls of corn
meant for hogs. Who forages the Soyanna's ravine
for nettles, sorrel, bear onion, club moss. Who at night
spoon-feeds her fevered sister earthen broth,
bunk window cataracted with steam.

Of

the fevered sister who dreams
their father stands up from where he was shot. *Kulak!*
the commissar barked. *Run to the house,* Father says
in the dream, dusting chaff from his coat. *Tell Mama*
I'll be in for supper soon. Bloom of blood,
his burst heart, furls back into bud.

Of

Oma who sings, *If I had a thousand hearts,*
I'd give them all to you, after they open the cattle cars,
give spades to the men to bury their dead by the tracks.
Stop! a man sobs. *Stop singing at once!* Oma's voice,
Maria zu lieben, murmuration of Black Sea
starlings, waves of wings dusk-bronzed.

Of

the swineherd who holds her sister
in Arctic owl-light, a shawl of faint stars, listens
to White Sea wind. *When I die,* Oma said in the dark
car, *don't be sad – it means I found a way to trick Stalin.*
Cracked lips against vellus, she whispers Oma's song
in her sister's ear, *If flesh and hell battle,*
you are my shelter.

Of

Mama in her daughter's typhoid-dream.
Look at this mess! She must tidy up, unknots the tablecloth,
loaves back in the cupboard, sweeps shards of china
into the corner. She tongue-clucks her youngest hiding

on the porch, *Your red apple cheeks!* She breathes
the clove of her girl's unwashed hair,
reties her scarf –

there, there. You can't stay here;

we are dead. Then she pushes her out,
leans all her weight against the door.

IV

Let Them Rest

...dies illa
Solvet sæclum in favilla
– Dies Irae

SW 26 36 22 W2ND

Buckbrush, snowberry,
spear grass, prairie wool, fescue –
seeded by out-turned pockets, torn hems from the Steppes.

Styptic sky, astringent, cirrus, alkali rime on harrowed dirt.
A bachelor shack in the back forty.
Porch overgrown with caraganas,

pull yourself through the kitchen window,
glass shot out decades ago. Breathe the charnel reek,
the cracked-open casket of the nation's turn-of-the-century bullshit-
promises, adipose gleam of barley and wheat.

Hung over the kitchen door, blue bibbed overalls, grease stained knees.
Chewed-on rubber boots in the leaf-shaded entrance,
men's size eleven. Two sets.

Open the cupboard above the sink.
Mouse shit and Watkins cinnamon.
Red Rose tea. Can of Brunswick sardines.
Shelves lined with pages from *The Western Producer* dated April 4th, 1958,

headlines of Diefenbaker's landslide victory, postulant of Sir John A,
His cribbed expansionist speech: *A new vision! A new hope! A new soul!*
cocked and loaded for Arctic minerals.

Breathe deep the viral load: pollen, saliva, feces, avian and animal.
The fever sets in, undoes the tiny clasp,
hook and eye of your peripheral sight.
See them –

in a slick of kerosene light, brothers at the kitchen table.
Two plates. Two forks. Two knives. Pork grease. Heinz Beans.
Post-war Germans.

Tens, twenties, fifties – life-savings
squirrelled in Black Cat tobacco tins.
Three or four beef cattle. A chicken coop.

Wearing Mother's apron, the younger brother bakes bread and kuchen.
At night he sleeps as though still crouched in her womb.

Quarter of land. Calcerous loam, low yields, saline sloughs –
forage crops, alfalfa, wild rye. Stones.

Once a July they pack up their 1950 Deluxe DeSoto –
egg sandwiches, black coffee. Hair, brylcreamed.

They fish Last Mountain Lake for walleye, pike. Mostly weeds.
In a good year, a hotel meal at Arlington Beach.

No one writes –
parents, a sister, buried in old-world cinders of war.

After supper fetor – orange pekoe steam, curdled milk, pipe smoke.
Plates pushed aside, the older brother goes to the *gute Stube*,

gear shift groan of the brown leather recliner,
dry sough of last week's *Western Producer*.

Before washing dishes, the younger sits at the table with a mug of tea,
leans back in his chair, stretches his legs. Can't digest

the gut-hunch that he only knows love
by its lack.

Twenty years later this is where the older will find him.
In from calving, stinking of blood and yeast, he'll call

and there'll be silence –
brain aneurysm. Heart attack.

Head laying on grey Formica. Above, the Jagdstück cuckoo
they brought from Bottrop bursts –

swing of doors,
the happy couple twirl and twirl

in Black Forest filigree,
crowned with rifle and stag.

PSALM 22

Lay me in the dust of death
grind my bones to salt.
My heart, wax,
melts in my breast,
mouthful of potsherd,
cinereous tongue,
locked jaw.

℟ Lay me in the dust.

The puma stalks.
The coyotes circle,
their calls pull me to pieces,
offspring of scorned sons –
Ishmael and Esau,
Alex, Peter, Mikhail,
Larry Joseph.

℟ Lay me in the dust.

Rent from her womb
six weeks too soon,
Wednesday's child,
jaundice, lanugo,
my keen hardly human.
People will mock. People will mock.
People will mock.

℟ Lay me in the dust.

NE 36 19 23 W2ND

Two attic bedrooms, plaster and lathe, cotton candy pink, baby bird blue.
A wooden rocking chair, missing spindles. Torn-out
pages from *Little Red Riding Hood* –

hackles, incisors, the ravening wolf.

Master bedroom at the bottom of the stairwell. Dim. Cool. Lilac blooms
poke through the east window. Dust in the slant of late afternoon
light. Breathe deep. The smell of your mother

when you were a girl and napped in the nest of her
queen-sized bed. Beneath the metal frame and box spring,
a pair of calfskin leather baby shoes. Laces tied.

Do not touch anything –

let her sleep. But sleep won't come to her eyes,
Her right breast burns, mastitis, nipples cracked.
His arm heavy across her chest,
soft *puh* of his slumber on her neck.

All day the wolf at her back, stalks from room to room.
What big eyes you have – the better to see.
What big ears. What big teeth.
The better to tear inside,

and hear what you cannot say –
(all flesh is grass,
the flower falls, bury the baby in lilac
branches. June blossoms,
milk-soaked mouths).

Upstairs, the children dream, lashes flicker,
silver underside of poplar leaves. All day they pull
her dress, her legs, her arms, her hair, her sleeves.
Let her sleep,

but sleep won't come,
the newborn in a basket by her bed,
her hand on the baby's belly to feel
the small tide of breath

(all flesh is grass,
the flower falls, lower the baby
into the well. Mineral drink of her spit and salt.
She'd find her way back into your womb).

The wolf stalks room to room. Let her sleep,
but sleep won't come. Behind her eyelids,
the hatchlings who slipped
too soon between her thighs

(bird bones flensed,
a fine mobile, strung above her head,
quilled by moon).

PSALM 130

Chemical burnoff after frost,
cocklebur, clubroot spores,
flixweed, lamb's-quarters,

LibertyLink® patent fees,
canola seed treated
for flea beetles,

Longtrel™ for dandelion
and thistle. At night,
the wives sit,

shoulders hunched,
at kitchen tables,
divine

profit margins
with calculators and lines
of credit from Wells Fargo –

If south winds don't blow in waves
of diamondback moths. If winter kills

the pupae of bertha armyworms.
If sun. If rain.

If crop insurance premium rates.
If 25 bushels an acre to pay input costs.

At night, the wives wait.
They count their bones
as the moon pours out.

NE 10 36 22 W2ND

Canola, pulse, cereal, flax, the field
    northwest of the yard-site, past the shelterbelt
of unshaved evergreens,

            caraganas and buffalo beans growing
    through rusted machinery – grain cart and auger,
            pull-type swather circa 1984.

Canola, pulse, cereal, flax, brushed nap of stubble,
    GPS-tracked, factory-stamped seed rows,
clots of soil, desiccated scabs,

            claw marks from the heavy harrow
                        spreading last season's trash –
                                    straw, chaff.

Canola, pulse, cereal, flax, Roundup,
    anhydrous ammonia, nitrogen gas,
granular phosphorus, sulfur, potash,

            120 pounds per acre of wheat seed,
    broadleaf herbicide, fungicide, insecticide,
            glyphosate-resistant ragweed

in low-spots and sloughs.
            Contagion of snow geese,
their many-throated scream,
                                    a terrible forgetting –

this is where the boy felt the animal's wet-eyed stare,
coyote, fox, jackrabbit, badger.

This is where he followed tracks, set snares in estrus-scent
and molt, scat, shed fur.

This is where he lay, a deer's wallow of slender wheatgrass
blue grass, brome and sedge,

watched catkins lift in updrafts, soft rattle of aspens,
dozed in the heavy breath of bloom –

balsam, wolf willow, chokecherries, saskatoons.
This is where he came in sorrow

after his father made him shoot the horned owl perched
in the spruce north of the chicken coop.

No proof the owl killed chicks.

Now, this is where the man,
neck in the noose of profit margins and farm credit,

runs the Rome Plow, the bush disc,
clears scrub, rakes roots for forty more acres to seed next spring.

The owl's wingspan,
at least five feet, though it weighed no more

than what he could hold
in his ten-year-old palms. All feathers and fluff,

shadow and light. After dusk,
this is where the man watches the piled bush burn, remembers

the owl's yellow eyes. Hiss and snap of heat –
sap, leaves, hank of dew. Osteoache, the shrinking moon.

It's true what they say. We were warned:
everything will be swept away,
everything consumed. Winter-killed

perch, walleye, pike, white bellies,
slack flags. Thousands
washed ashore at Stoney Lake –

fertiliser run-off,
nitrogen, phosphorus,
blue-green algae bloom.

℟ It's true. We were warned.

Everything swept away.
Everything consumed. Sky bled dry
of midges. Locusts, bees, neurons frayed.

Antiseptic silence of canola
fields at dusk, muted
grasshopper thrum.

℟ Our blood poured out like dust.

Swept away. Consumed.
Empty Barn Swallow nests
in rafters and eaves.

The Western Meadowlark's throat,
an open grave. Neonic-coated
soybean, canola, sunflower, wheat.

White Crown Sparrows,
migration delayed,
anorexic, compass lost.

℟ A land possessed of nettles and salt.

Ferruginous Hawk,
Black-tailed Prairie Dog,
Bobolink, longspurs, pipits,

Swift Fox, Whip-por-whirl,
Piping Plover, Whooping Crane,
Sage Grouse. We were warned:

fish, fowl, animal.
And they who weigh silver,
merchants and traders?

NW 18 44 22 W2ND

Clothesline droops with the ghost of wet sheets,
translucent moth wings. Ghost moth larvae feed on burdock
in Mrs Rochinsky's overgrown garden, quack grass, chickweed.

You used to come here,
tried on the left-behind dresses of the dead. Butterick patterns.
Tiny purple flowers. Mrs Rochinsky's sweat-stained milk vetch.

Kitchen door, off the hinges,
in thigh-high brome, a rotten tooth. Someone will pull this root –
knock down the house and yard for five more acres to seed.

Talons hooked over the lintel,
Mrs Rochinsky's arthritic fingers, curled in earth.
Ravens croak: *You were warned.*

GREAT PLAINS AUCTIONS

With food in our throats, we asked for more.
With food in our mouths, we still asked for more.
There was meat and bread, but our craving unslaked.
Fat gardens, braids of onion, bled heifers and pigs,
skinned, scalded, scraped.

Sure, we were sad to see our neighbours go,
bid extra on their socket sets, air compressors
leftover five-gallon pails of hydraulic oil.
Sold! the auctioneer's speakers
rattled in his truckbed.

We told ourselves, if they could, they'd do the same.
Frost out of the ground, we poured red froth,
Vitamax®, into our auger boxes of churning seed.
To stop stinking smut, *C. Sativus*, root rot.
Soil borne disease.

You will build houses
you don't inhabit,

plant crops
you don't eat.

Your reckless prophets,
hungry wolves,

will leave
nothing.

NW 18 36 22 W2ND

Gather in the summer fallowed south field.
Winter-stiff furrows. No moon. No snow.
Overcast. Hold hands.

Farm subsidies smashed by Intercontinental Packers,
Big Sky Pork Farms. Our barns now their finishing
pens for 10 000 pigs from 1000 sows.

No moon. No snow. No yard-lights for miles,
like an eye put out. Hold hands. We are
but breath, but chaff, what passes
and does not come again.

OLD ST BENEDICT CHURCH, RM OF HOODOO

Where beeswax, chrism, myrrh.
Where teething babies on mother-laps
pulled and sucked fistfuls of faux pearl.
Where we held out our tongues for bread.
Where dust circled in stained-light.
Where cradles. Where coffins.
Where holy water rained.

Black mould climbs the walls, trapped breath of petitions.

A choir of short horn grasshoppers.
A choir of katydids.
A choir of wind.

The cantor sings: *Let me begin again ~*

This was our new heaven. This was our new earth,
where our former homes were forgotten.

Outside ataxic mule deer stutter between
mossed and dated stones. Our bones
in the loam-womb, the dirt
of our new Jerusalem.

THE PARISH OF ST SCHOLASTICA
ERECTED THIS MONUMENT
IN MEMORY OF THOSE BURIED HERE
1976

Bernadette Blanch – 1 year
George Blanch – 7 years
Jacob Grunsky – 1857-1918
Margaret Koppes – 1924
Anna & Regina Lorenz – infant twins
Frieda Lorenz – 1925
Leonard Lorenz – July 13, 1935
Peter Lukonowsky – 1911
Makarewicz Baby
Martin Novecosky – Sept. 1909
Elizabeth Novecosky – Jan. 1925
Katherine Roschinsky – June 30, 1918
Katherine Roschinsky – June 29, 1920
Child of J. Roschinksy
Jacob Saretsky – Feb. 6, 1911
Rudolph Saretsky – 1923
Maria Magdalena Saretsky – 1924
Ann Saretsky – 4 months
Bergetta Saretsky – 6 weeks
Child of B. Saretsky – Oct. 15 1942
Josephine Schedlosky – Feb. 1909
Katherine Schedlosky – Dec. 1918
Clara Scheiber – Sept. 1912
Leona Schikowski – Feb. 29, 1936
Joseph Suchan – June 1920
Elizabeth Suchan – June 1920
Elizabeth Suchan – Feb. 1922
Bernard Suchan – Mar. 1922
Frank Joseph Suchan – Aug. 1922
Child of M. Zubot

THE PARISH OF ST SCHOLASTICA
ERECTED THIS MONUMENT
IN MEMORY OF THOSE BURIED HERE
1976

Umbilical twist, forehead to forehead, sea-lily fingers on each other's cheeks, Mrs. Lorenz's skinned rabbits, born breech. *Heal, heal, bless.* The doctor said he could not staunch her bleed. Placental hemorrhage. *Heal, heal, bless.* Martin Merkowsky's dangling whip, yanked by his dog and caught in the axle. *Heal, heal, bless.* His great grandson thrown from his pickup in dun-feathered dawn. Coyote fur, November frost and straw. *Heal, heal, bless.* Magdalena drowned from weeping for the baby she sowed in the Baltic's silver furrows. *Heal, heal, bless.* Ann and Bergetta, Katherine and Katherine, Child of M. Zubot: fever-faced, musk thistle. *Heal, heal, bless.* Ronnie Suchan's trigger pin worn loose on his rifle, winter rosehip below his left eyebrow. *Heal, heal, bless.* Richard Benning, mid-harvest, wheat kernels in armpits, calyx cracked, non-Hodgkin's lymphoma. *Heal, heal, bless.* Late August frogs and grasshoppers sang to Jack Ritz, face-first in dirt, while the grain bin crushed him. *Heal, heal, bless.* Diseases in dialect: *A'Wachse* (livergrown), *Hergeschperr* (lockedheart), *Alpricke'* (when the night witch sits on your chest). *Heal, heal, bless.* Morphine drip, dehydration, fetal-curled in the care home, St Mary's Villa. *Heal, heal, bless.*

Mother, Mother,
blow on the slivered finger, the bruised knee.
Three days rain. Three days snow.
Tomorrow it won't hurt anymore.
Heal, heal, bless.

THE PARISH OF ST SCHOLASTICA
ERECTED THIS MONUMENT
IN MEMORY OF THOSE BURIED HERE
1976

St Scholastica's Fall Supper, six feet deep in the earth.
Sod ceiling drips pesticide leach, bones laced with malathion,
2,4-D, turnip smell of canola and stinkweed,
wild oats and kochia roots tangled in hair.

Don't mention the cutworms
that chew dresses and best denims.

Parishioners, we paid our fees to feast, tossed 30 pieces
on the temple floor, the Dominion Lands Act, 1872, proved up
on our field of blood, 160 acres of Oxbow sandy loam.
Cheekbones and mandibles gleam. Mothers give
toddlers drumsticks to gnaw,
cartilage and marrow.

Don't mention the bread was salted with tears.
Don't mention the bowlfuls and bowlfuls of tears.

Parishioners, push back your chairs!
Bring out the accordion! Waltz and polka,
turn and turn. Your bones knit rich dirt. Sated babies
snooze on half-moons of mother-shoulders.

Don't mention the tremble, the 700 horsepower John Deere
overhead, the tank tread, the stretching bellows, the thickening drone –

My ghost waits for me here.

V

et lux perpétua lúceat eis ~

FEAST

Chokecherries, spider webs,
slough water spiced with lilac,
spear grass, cattails, caragana pods.
Farm debt. Drought. The locust drone
of adult-talk. *Girls, come in for lunch.*

Ignore her cries. Rhubarb stalks
dipped in stolen sugar. Shelled peas,
carrots from the garden, dirt shaken off.
Our table set in the smoulder of sage,
river scent of wolf willow shade.

VIATICUM

Psalm 42

These things I remember: the light
in crested wheat, spear grass, meadow brome,
the pasture's first baize flush, late April.

When tears are my meat day and night:
metal on metal echo in the farmyard,
late afternoon. Oil-stained coveralls,

he's fixing tines on the heavy harrow
while she sweeps grain bins for truckloads
of bulk-seed – flax, barley, oats, peas –

sweet smell of last harvest's rotting crop.
Sun low, barn cats grappling by the fuel tanks,
air cooled by melting snow.

When they ask, *where is your place?* the slough
in the field west of our barns, stubble and dirt
loosened from frost, furred willows,

frog chorus, the coyotes' dusk antiphonal,
a bell's tongue in bone marrow. These things
I remember as I pour out my soul.

WINTER SLEEP

1 *Kings* 19

Leather belt tight around my chest,
sackcloth of barley itch, I wake
in a camel-hair nest,

foxtail, buffalo berry, crested wheat,
leaf-mould, a grotto of poplars
at the foot of a hill, Kisipatinaw,

renamed Mount Carmel
in the *Geological Survey of Canada,* 1873.
Mouth dry, I eat what ravens leave.

Blood-warm sun, wild honey
in my eyes, chaff shimmer,
locust buzz, the pilgrims arrive

for the Rosary Crusade, September 26th 1948.
Drone of the Sorrowful Mysteries,
cousins, uncles, aunties, yoked

by sweat-worn beads, process
up the hill behind Abbot Severin OSB.
Lashes flicker, cabbage butterflies,

behind eyelids they carry
the blue of the Black Sea, ripe plums,
Pontic steppe tilth. I run to them,

tug dress hems, shirtsleeves,
but they can't open their eyes for fear
of losing all that salt, sugar, dirt.

At the top of the hill,
beneath the statue of Mary
(marble imported from Italy)

Abbot Severin lifts
the Blessed Sacrament into the sea
of sky. Horizon to horizon,

fields in stook and stubble.
Stones fill the well of my throat.
Parasomnic, I can't breathe –

Where coyotes licked the blood
of those whose land you broke,
they'll lick yours –

but no one turns. No one believes.
We were told the jar of meal
would not empty. Oil would not fail.

After Holy Communion they picnic
on cold chicken and jelly, rosehip, chokecherry.
In my dream, I wake while most still sleep.

TO GLASGOW

Standing on the platform, Manchester Victoria,
waiting for the after supper train. Home,
to Glasgow.

Spring sky, bruised fruit. Pigeons in eaves.
Rain-bloated newsprint, overripe peonies
that lined the porch at the farm,
long sold.

A breeze lifts my hair, sweat of my nape,
a train, not mine, shoots past. Diesel,
smoke from the burn barrel at dusk,
the farm again,

dew on bluestem, my body, my breath. My face
in the windows of passing cars. *I am. I am.*
There is no going back.

NOTES

Let Them Rest
'Vast and worthless', and 'an ocean with no past', are a couple of descriptions of the Great Plains grasslands by early European explorers. The inability of newcomers to 'see' the prairies engendered efforts to 'improve' the land, to channel its energy into the production of commodities. One such effort, farming, took phenomenal hold. See Candace Savage's, *Prairie: A Natural History.*

The Dominion Lands Act effectively granted free land to settlers as part of a process that displaced Indigenous and Métis peoples from their traditional homes. Farmers were given 160 acres for a $10 administrative fee contingent on their cultivation of at least 40 acres and the building of a permanent dwelling on it within three years. The requirement that farmers 'prove up the homestead' was established to preclude the land being bought by speculators.

By 1913 a million people had settled the prairies, reined in by Ottawa's grid system of land division that disregarded harmonising with the natural terrain.

In recent years, the diversified family farm has given way to agribusiness and intensive farming practices. The average farm size has tripled; there are now 50,000 fewer farms than there were fifty years ago. As farms increase in size, land and community suffer. Beyond Saskatchewan's cities, you'll find abandoned yards and town sites even as the most vulnerable prairie terrain is pressed into cultivation. 'Let Them Rest' visits this wrecked farmscape. Some places' names have been changed.

The manuscript's epigraph is from Jan Zwicky's poem 'Depth', published in *The Long Walk* by University of Regina Press, 2016.

The line 'Blessed is the field as it burns' in 'All of it' is borrowed from Brigit Pegeen Kelly's poem 'Blessed is the Field', published in *Song and The Orchard* by Carcanet Press, 2008.

The final stanza of 'Compline', reworks lines from Jan Zwicky's poem 'Kinderszenen', published in *Forge* by Gaspereau Press, 2011.

The epigraph for part three is from Evan Boland's poem 'First Year', published in *Code* by Carcanet Press, 2001.

LIST OF ILLUSTRATIONS

Photo credits: Heather Benning

ACKNOWLEDGEMENTS

Some of these poems first appeared in *The Paris Review*, *Times Literary Supplement*, *PN Review*, *Poetry Review*, *The Manchester Review*, *The Glasgow Review of Books*, *Prairie Fire*, and *Grain*. My heartfelt thanks to the editors.

The seed of this manuscript was planted years ago in Tim Lilburn's philosophy classes at St Peter's College in Muenster, Saskatchewan. Tim, I'm grateful for your help with the poems and for our continued conversation. I'm also grateful for Jan Zwicky's invaluable insight and support.

Warmest thanks to Michael Schmidt, John McAuliffe, Andrew Latimer, Jazmine Linklater and everyone at Carcanet Press.

For the sustaining conversation which made this manuscript possible, thank you Heather Benning and Fraser Duncan, as well as William Bartley, Dianne Chisholm, Laurie D. Graham, Michael Helm, Barbara Langhorst, Sylvia Legris, Jeanette Lynes, Rev. Paul Paproski OSB, Karen Solie, Jen Tindall, and Guy Vanderhaege.

Thank you Chad Galloway and Heather Benning for our collaboration on the short film *Winter Sleep* based on my poem of the same name. I'm grateful to Sarah Ens, Laurie D. Graham, Carolyn Gray, Sylvia Legris, Andrea McCrimmon, Geoff Pevlin, William Robertson, and Guy Vanderhaege for lending their voices.

Conversations with Larry and Rosalie Benning were more than crucial to these poems. Thank you is not enough. This book is for you, and for Kurt and Heather. *NW* 18 36 22 *W2nd.*

'Pentecost' is for Rosalie Benning.

'Kelly Wiens' is for Cara, Carla, Christine, Faye, Lindsay, Lynn, Terri, Trina, and our Kelly.

'Of, the swineherd' is for Sarah Ens.

'Feast' is for Heather Benning.